JON BLAKE

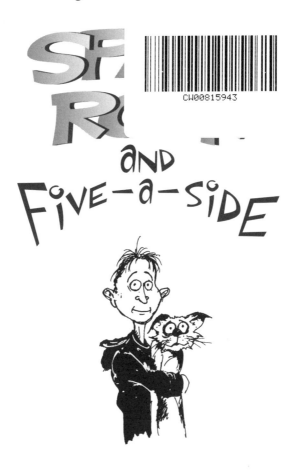

AND
Five-a-Side

Illustrated by Chris Mould

OXFORD
UNIVERSITY PRESS

OXFORD
UNIVERSITY PRESS

Great Clarendon Street, Oxford OX2 6DP

Oxford University Press is a department of the University of Oxford.
It furthers the University's objective of excellence in research, scholarship,
and education by publishing worldwide in

Oxford New York
Auckland Bangkok Bogotá Buenos Aires
Cape Town Chennai Dar es Salaam Delhi Hong Kong Istanbul
Karachi Kolkata Kuala Lumpur Madrid Melbourne Mexico City Mumbai
Nairobi São Paulo Shanghai Taipei Tokyo Toronto

Oxford is a trade mark of Oxford University Press
in the UK and in certain other countries

British Library Cataloguing in Publication Data
Data available

ISBN 0 19 915965 3

Printed in the UK by Goodmanbaylis

Available in packs

Year 6/ Primary 7 Pack of Six (one of each book) ISBN 0 19 915971 8
Year 6 / Primary 7 Class Pack (six of each book) ISBN 0 19 915972 6

Contents

Preface: Batcat

It is my great ambition to play football for England. At the moment, however, I can't make the Stegg End School five-a-side reserve team.

Despite the fact that I am brilliant.

There are two reasons for this.

One, (according to Mr Bollom) is that I am no good at reading the game. Reading about the game, maybe, but not reading the game. And two, Cornel hates me. Cornel is captain. He has never forgiven me for that blinding shot I cracked last year. That shot was destined to speed ten metres and break the back netting. Unfortunately, Cornel got in the way. He was roughly ten centimetres from my boot at the time. I'm not sure how much damage it caused, but his face did wear a spectacular expression and his voice also changed for a while.

I would do anything to get in that team, especially now the Schools' Cup is upon us. Winning the Schools' Cup means everything. You stand in front of everyone at assembly, your picture is in the paper, and you drive through Wallingford in an open-top bus with people hanging out of the windows cheering. Almost.

Meanwhile, I sit in my bedroom next to a dingy table lamp and play with Batcat.

Batcat is the family cat. She is called Batcat because of her great black ears. Batcat is a tortoiseshell, a riot of black, white, and orange, with black eyeliner round both eyes and a ginger tip to her tail. Her favourite habit is to drag a spare rib bone out of the bin-bag then run through to the living room to devour it. Mum always has a fit when she does this, and… (I'm taking a long time to get into the story, aren't I? Never mind, it is coming. Eventually.)...she slings the nearest object at her. I mean Mum does.

Meanwhile, Batcat makes a beeline for my bedroom. Why, you ask? Simple. Because I let her crunch her bones in peace. As far as I'm concerned, Batcat is a wild animal. She never invented the rules about polite eating. I say, let nature be nature. Except, in Batcat's case, I'm not exactly sure what her nature is.

She's always had an odd look in her eye, not like a cat at all. That's why we picked her, you see. Calum Casey organized a kitten race for his cat's kittens – all six of them. He made a track out of old planks, put food down one end and the kittens down at the other. Then he went "Go!" and clapped two saucepans together.

The kittens went off like thunder-crackers. All except Batcat, who lazily stretched her tiny leg and licked that place which cats so love to lick. When Calum screamed at her she looked very calmly at him and I'll swear she raised one eyebrow.

At that moment, I knew she was the cat for us.

There was another thing which made me think Batcat was different. It was the way she watched me when I was working at my PC. Oh yes, I do work. Work at improving my score on Star Fighter 2, mainly. Anyway, it seemed strangely fascinating to Batcat. Then, one night… (I really am taking a long time to get on with my story, aren't I? But I've just got to tell you this bit.)

Well, one night, something disturbed my sleep. As I opened my eyes I became aware of a misty blue light and the sound of soft tapping. At first the light seemed all around me, but as I sat up, I realized it was coming from the corner of the room.

My eyes focussed. I saw that my PC was

switched on, even though I was sure I had turned it off. On the screen were all kinds of characters and a complicated graph. And there, sitting before it, pattering at the keys, was Batcat.

Almost without thinking, I threw myself out of bed and went towards her. Her head flicked round, her paw stabbed the 'off' switch and next instant she was gone.

I turned the PC back on but nothing was

saved. Heart thumping, I searched the house for her. No Batcat, so I gave up and went back to bed.

Next morning, when I woke up, everything looked normal and I began to wonder if I had dreamed the whole episode.

Over the next few days I made several attempts to catch Batcat in the act again. I deliberately left her in the room with the PC on, and watched for hours through the keyhole. I set my alarm watch for the middle of the night. I put graphs on the screen and turned round suddenly to try to catch her watching.

None of it worked. I became more and more convinced that it had been a dream. But I did notice one thing. Batcat caught four mice that week, at least twice as many as usual. It was just as if she had used a program to plan it.

Where was I? Ah yes, the story. Right, here goes:

Once upon a time... No, that's a rubbish start.

It came to pass, in the town of Wallingfor... That sounds like the Bible.

Nicky-Nacky-Wicky-Wacky...

That's original.

Yes, I think I'll start with that.

1
Nicky-Nacky-Wicky-Wacky

Nicky-Nacky-Wicky-Wacky. This was the song my dad liked to sing every morning. No tune, but bags of volume. Dad woke up very, very early and he liked to make sure the rest of us shared the joy of the morning with him.

After the song came the humungous crunch of his cornflakes and the *tink, tink, tink,* of spoon against bowl. Then there was his trip to the toilet, which went on for so long it sounded like seven baths being run. Finally, there was the car being started, which took even longer, and sounded like twelve coughing dogs going round in a spin-drier.

Dad got up early because he worked on the bins. This confused me, because everyone else who worked on the bins lived in council houses or little terraces. We lived in a big private house on Herby Park Lake and had a telly in every room. We moved there quite suddenly three years ago. At the same time, Dad started working some unusually long shifts. Sometimes he wouldn't be back for three or four days. Often when he did come back, he found it difficult to adjust to being home and would sit for hours in the garden staring at the stars. Mum wasn't the type to ask questions, and told us Dad was probably having a MID-LIFE CRISIS, whatever that was.

It was during one of Dad's joyful mornings that my adventure began.

"Joseph?"

That's my name. Dad was crouched down at the side of my bed in his work cap and donkey jacket, looking urgently towards my face.

"It's… half past six!" I grunted.

"Time to get up," said Dad.

"Uh?"

"This morning," said Dad, "you're coming with me."

*   *   *

As we drove through the bleary, half-awake streets, Dad began a serious conversation. Dad didn't find it easy to talk like this, and kept his eyes firmly fixed on the road ahead.

"Have you considered," he said, "what you might be when you grow up?"

"A professional footballer," I replied.

There was an awkward silence.

"Not many boys get to achieve that ambition," said Dad.

"Some do," I replied.

Another awkward silence.

"It's good to have dreams," said Dad, "but it's also good to keep your feet on the ground."

"Except when you're going for headers," I replied.

"Sorry?" said Dad.

"Not that you get many headers in five-a-side," I continued. "The ball must remain below shoulder level. Unless, of course, you're playing *outdoor* five-a-side, which is a different matter altogether."

I'd lost Dad completely. He took a breath and tried again. "Have you ever considered," he asked, "following in your father's footsteps?"

"On the bins?" I replied.

"Why not?" said Dad. "It's an important job. And a steady income."

"Some Manchester United players get more than £30,000 a week," I pointed out.

"So do I," said Dad.

"What?" I replied.

"I'm not an ordinary binman you know," said Dad.

My eyes narrowed. "What are you then?" I asked.

"You'll find out soon enough," replied Dad.

2

The Star Cart

The council depot looked ordinary enough.
Rows and rows of refuse vans, two big skips
marked FOR PUBLIC USE and NOT FOR
PUBLIC USE, and a dull red building marked
STAFF ONLY. We went in there. Dad clocked
on, then walked into the staff canteen. The
other workers looked up but no one said
hello. We sat at a table on our own, waiting
for Charlie, who was Dad's driver.

"Dad," I asked. "Why is no one speaking
to you?"

"Jealousy," replied Dad.

"What are they jealous of?" I asked.

"You'll find out soon enough," said Dad.

I sat there feeling very embarrassed, knowing people were watching me and wondering why I was there. I would have told them if I'd known myself.

Charlie arrived. He was a square-shaped man with a flat, leathery face and a hangover. No one said hello to him either, not even Dad.

"Better be off," said Dad.

"Another day, another dollar," said Charlie.

We trudged out into the yard, past the waiting trucks, towards a dull, silvery building like a gigantic shed, with nothing but the number seven on it.

"This is Joseph, by the way," said Dad.

"Oh," said Charlie.

We reached the shed. Dad's fingers hovered over the security lock.

"Er..." he muttered, "when did England win the World Cup?"

"1966, Dad."

"1966. That's the one."

Dad tapped out the four numbers. The lock was released, a door slid open, and we walked into the building. In front of us was an incredible sight. The entire building was filled by a monster refuse truck.

It was five times the size of the others, with STAR CART blazed along its length in mighty red letters. Oh, and one other thing. It was standing on its end.

"Woah!" I cried.

Charlie and Dad didn't seem so impressed. "Better get the gear on," mumbled Dad. Hanging on the wall were three sets of overalls. They were the same green colour as normal council overalls, but much shinier, and puffier, with a big pack on the back.

"These are a bit flash," I said, climbing into mine.

"Wait till you see the helmet," said Dad.

"Helmet?" I replied.

Dad reached up into a nearby rack and took down something like an outsize goldfish bowl. There was a mirror-glass visor on the front and WALLINGFORD COUNCIL REFUSE DEPT on the back. Dad pulled the helmet over his head and attached it to the overalls with an airtight seal.

"Dad!" I cried. "You look like a spaceman!"

Dad laid a hand on my shoulder. When he spoke, it was in a distant voice like a cheap radio. "Son," he said, "I *am* a spaceman."

I stared back at his helmet but all I saw was my own amazed expression. Dad, a spaceman? This was unthinkable!

"But...why?" I asked.

"As you know," said Dad, "space is full of rubbish. Disused satellites, broken solar panels, lost screwdrivers. Someone's got to clear it up."

"But why you?" I asked.

"Mr Reliable, that's me," said Dad. "Not like the first ones they sent up."

"Why?" I asked. "What were they like?"

"Oh, you know," said Dad. "The pushy ones. The go-getters. They didn't last long."

"Why not?"

"Can't tell you that, son. Top secret."

"Can we get a move on?" said Charlie.

"Affirmative," said Dad.

* * *

I know what you're thinking. Space dustmen? How come no one's seen them? How come the other binmen don't talk about them?

I assure you there are good answers to these questions. If you don't believe me, well, you can stop reading, can't you? It's no skin off my nose. I'm just about to go into space.

* * *

We made our way into the Star Cart and strapped ourselves into the cockpit. This was very much like the front seat of a van, except much bigger, with a computer where the radio cassette should be, covered in old fag ends and sweet wrappers. Dad told me not to worry, because Charlie was an old hand who knew exactly what he was doing.

Meanwhile Charlie was frantically fishing about in his pockets. "Where did I put those stupid keys?" he said.

"You left them in the ignition," said Dad.

"Blow me."

Charlie unlocked the crooklock and turned on the engine. There was a sound like Dad's old Ford, except echoing round the Grand Canyon.

"She's a devil to start on a cold morning," said Charlie.

"Give it some choke, Charlie," said Dad.

Charlie tried again. There was a deep bass roar far below us. The roof parted, then I had a most peculiar feeling, like an invisible elephant was sitting on my face. I didn't even realize we were moving, till clouds scudded past the front window and the deep blackness of space beckoned. Everything was rattling and banging like a clown's car, and Charlie hung on to the wheel like grim death.

Then the blackness was all around, and things quietened. We were actually in space. Lots of space. Dad and Charlie started to prattle on about neutron phasers and Warp Sectors and all that *Star Trek* gobbledegook, but I don't think it meant anything. They were just trying to impress me.

"Right," said Dad, eventually. "Let's get out."

"Out?" I repeated, nervously.

"Can't collect rubbish sitting here, can we?"

Dad took off his seat belt and I was surprised to see him gently float into the air. He swam to the rear of the cockpit and uncoiled two long silver tubes. He attached one to the front of my suit and one to his own.

I took off my seat belt and joined him in mid-air. He led me through a door into the exit bay. The bay door opened and we tumbled into space. Only those thin silver tubes prevented us from floating off into distant space forever.

"Now, son," said Dad, in that unearthly radio voice, "Do you remember that time I told you not to play football near the house?"

"Yes, Dad?"

"And you ignored me, and broke the window?"

"Yes, Dad?"

Suddenly Dad took hold of my lifeline.

"I was going to stop your pocket money," he said, "but I have decided to do this instead."

With that, Dad unclipped the line from my suit and waved goodbye. I watched myself, reflected in Dad's visor, floating helplessly away into the nothingness.

Only joking.

It did cross my mind, though, as we pawed our way along the outside of the Star Cart. It could have happened. After all, as I've said, I never really knew Dad at all. If he could keep quiet about being a spaceman, who knows what else was going on in his head?

At the rear of the cart was a metal step and

some handgrips. That's where we rode, just like regular binmen, except half-way to the Moon.

It wasn't long before our first piece of rubbish appeared. I got really excited about this, but Dad said it was just another old weather satellite and slung it straight in the back.

The Star Cart chewed it up like a liquorice allsort.

Next came a discarded fuel tank. Dad checked it over carefully, then scowled.

"Typical," he said. "Those skinflints at NASA never leave a tip."

We chucked the fuel tank in the back, then smacked our hands, as if to say good riddance.

Nothing came along for the next thousand miles or so, then we passed by the Shangri-La Space Station. Just beneath, there was a whole load of leftovers tied up in a black bag. As usual, something had got into the bag and left rubbish strewn all down the space-lane.

I don't want to talk about what came next. All you need to know is that space stations have toilets, but space doesn't have drains.

"Right," said Dad, checking his watch. "Tea break."

We sat down on the step and relaxed. Dad fished into his suit and brought out a packet of crumpets, which he toasted in the rocket-stream on the end of a screwdriver. Food always tastes great in the open air, and even better in space.

"So," said Dad. "How about following in your old dad's footsteps? It's not a bad life, is it?"

"Hmm," I said. "Didn't you say I should keep my feet on the ground?"

"Did I say that?" asked Dad.

"Your exact words, Dad," I replied.

"But you must admit," said Dad, "it's a nice job."

"Brilliant," I said, "apart from everyone else hating you."

"Apart from that, yes."

I looked out into the stars. "Dad," I said. "Do you ever wonder what would happen if you just kept on going? Would the universe go on forever, or would you get to the end of it? And if you did get to the end of it... what then?"

It was the kind of question I was always asking, and Dad so loved to avoid.

"Wonder if Mum's paid the gas?" he mused.

3

Space Rock

The fact is, we could have had a tea break for the next five hours and it wouldn't have made any difference. The space rubbish was very thin on the ground.

Then, out of the blue, something magical happened. We were just about to climb back into the cart when a shower of meteorites came towards us. They were coral pink and glowed like little suns.

"Wow!" I said.

"Leave 'em," said Dad.

"Why?"

"Just leave 'em."

I dived in a beautiful arc off the back of the cart, and caught a space rock like a slow-motion slip fielder. It snuggled into my glove like a currant bun.

"Joseph!" said Dad. "What did I just tell you?"

"Just wanted to play with it, Dad!"

"Throw it away!"

It's bad enough being ordered around at home, let alone in outer space. I vaguely wondered if parents were in charge everywhere in the universe or just on Earth. Then I did as I was told and released the space rock. It didn't really matter. Especially as I'd caught another one behind my back with my other hand.

On the way back home we sang a few songs and Charlie even cracked a joke about needing a new fan belt. At least I think it was a joke. You were never quite sure with Charlie. He kept the same straight face no matter what was going on – even when the Earth suddenly loomed up on the windscreen, so blue and beautiful it made me gasp.

"Dangerous business, re-entry," he mumbled.

"Why's that?" I asked.

"Got to get the angle right," he explained.

"Like a goalie?" I suggested.

"That's right," said Charlie. "Except if a goalie gets the angle wrong, he lets in a goal. If I get it wrong, we die."

I waited for Charlie to smirk or wink or nudge me in the ribs. But he kept on talking in the same dull monotone: "Get the angle too steep, we burn up. Get the angle too flat, we bounce off into space... forever."

I looked to Dad. He simply nodded. At this point I firmly closed my eyes and did not open them again till we were securely back in the council depot.

4
Little Secrets

Back home, Dad took me into the garage for a serious talk.

"No one is to know about your trip to space," he said. "It'll be our little secret."

Sharing a secret with Dad seemed almost exciting. At the same time it made me anxious.

"Do you think it's right," I said, "keeping secrets from Mum?"

"Sometimes secrets are necessary," replied Dad.

"That's all right, then," I said, feeling the

lump in my pocket.

* * *

I made sure the bedroom door was securely
locked before I took out
the space rock. I
placed it carefully
on the desk and
studied it from all
angles. I can hardly
explain the thrill I
was feeling, but it
basically broke down
into three parts:

1 Knowing the rock came from beyond the
   Earth.
2 The eerie pink glimmer.
3 The fact that Dad had told me not to
   take it.

I tested the rock for smell. Its scent was faint,
yet strangely powerful. It reminded me of
sherbet and the first day of spring, with just a
hint of swimming baths. Hmm, I thought to
myself. I wonder how it tastes? Cautiously,

my tongue crept from my mouth... closer... closer...

"Joseph! What are you doing in there!"

Mum!

With fumbling fingers I ushered the space rock into the top drawer of my desk, covered it with a footy magazine, and shut the drawer tight.

* * *

Next day was a big day for me. There was a games period first thing and Mr Bollom would be taking us for five-a-side. The team for the Schools' Cup (round one) would get picked the same morning.

I did my usual rituals. I laid out my kit with the trainers at the top, muttered a quick prayer to my poster of Inter Milan and tickled Batcat seven times under the chin. Then something occurred to me. If I needed luck, what could be better than the space rock?

I took the rock out of the drawer. I laid my hand on it and closed my eyes. Somehow, I knew it wasn't enough. A voice inside me was screaming, "Taste it! Taste it!" So this time I poked out my tongue, and I did.

It tasted good. Quite spicy, but not exactly like anything you could name. Some of the grains came off on my tongue, and without thinking, I swallowed them. Almost immediately my confidence seemed to grow. A daring feeling came over me.

I scratched off some more of the rock and swallowed that as well. Now I've got space magic inside me, I thought to myself.

I set off for school feeling ready for anything. I wasn't sure if it was all in my mind, or if something had happened to my body, but I was cool, relaxed, in control of things. At first it was quite a small, good feeling, but by the time I reached the school gates it was a humungous, elephant-sized good feeling. I ran up to my mate Daniel, pounced, and wrestled him to the ground.

"What's up?" he said

"Space," I said.

I couldn't wait to get in that gym with a ball at my feet. And when I did, and the game started, I was cooking. I wouldn't say I was more skilful with my feet, but my head was as clear as day, and that's what counted. I could see what was about to happen, I knew where to move, and I had a sixth sense of where my team-mates were.

Within ten minutes we were five up. I'd made the first four and scored the fifth, clinically, without a moment's doubt. As the game wore on, so my control tightened. I was the Playmaker. Everything flowed through me. I was David Beckham and Pele all rolled into one.

In the last minute, I body-swerved past Neil Cowley, took the entire defence left, then sent a perfect diagonal pass to the right wing. Cornel couldn't fail to tap it in. As the final whistle blew, I offered him a high five. He blanked me.

"Well played, Georgie," he said to George Dawson who hadn't done anything in particular.

Mr Bollom, however, was well impressed. "Hey, Joe," he said. "What did you have for breakfast?"

"Nothing special," I replied. Then I launched into this incredible discussion of game-plans and tactics, and 3-5-2 versus 4-4-2, which set Mr Bollom off on one of his nostalgic rants about 4-3-3, 4-2-4 and even 2-3-5. Then I went on to the virtues of playing a man in the hole, which started Mr Bollom off on the continental sweeper system. By the time we'd finished everyone was dressed and gone, break was over and I couldn't remember a thing I'd been talking about.

That lunchtime, the team-sheet was up and mine was the first name on it.

5

A Sea of Doubts

When I got home that afternoon I felt restless and irritable. I didn't want the action to stop, and now that it had, a sea of doubts swept over me. Would I bottle it when I played for the school? Would Cornel ever like me?

I always pretended I hated Cornel, but the truth was, I admired him. Cornel was a natural leader. When the team was up, he slapped people's backs and when the team was down, he never gave up. The gym echoed with the sound of his voice, geeing people up, urging them forward, marshalling the defence. Cornel wasn't afraid to praise a good tackle, or condemn a bad shot. People wanted to please him. And now I actually had the chance, I realized I wanted to please him as well.

I took out the space rock and studied it again. I replayed eating it, and the feeling that grew over me. That wasn't just coincidence. The space rock had done it for me. And it could do it again.

The trouble was, I didn't know what else it might do to me. What if I suddenly went blind, or came out in a purple rash, or woke up with no toes? As usual when I was in doubt, I whistled for Batcat.

Batcat sat on the desk, and I studied her face. It was incredible, that face. She was like a pharaoh, a Queen of the Nile,

with her black-lined eyes and her fierce, ancient face.

Batcat had the wisdom of centuries in her. She always knew what to do.

I placed the space rock beneath her nose. She studied it for a moment, sniffed it, then turned away and jumped off the desk. As she did this she brushed the space rock with the ginger tip of her tail.

"That's it!" I said to myself. "That's a sign it's all right!"

The truth was, that was just what I wanted to think.

6
Mad for It

When the day of the match came around, nerves really got hold of me. I couldn't afford to take any chances. I borrowed one of Mum's nail files and filed a small pile of space rock on to a sheet of paper.

Hmm, I thought to myself. If a tiny mouthful made me brilliant, what would a big mouthful do for me? I filed some more, then more again. I looked at the shimmering pink pyramid of powder and drew a deep breath. Then I licked the lot up.

Half-way to school the space rock was

already taking effect. The nerves had gone and a beautiful calm feeling had taken over. Everything was going to be just fine.

As I reached school, however, the feeling was beginning to change. Calm self-confidence had grown into raging self-belief. At the sight of a football in the playground I could not control myself.

I bolted like a bull terrier into the middle of the game, dragged the ball back under my foot, shimmied past two defenders and curled the ball into the top corner of the bike shed. Then I ran back past the startled kids (average age seven), arms outstretched, palms upwards, face contorted like Maradona when he scored in that World Cup.

That wasn't the end of it. The feeling kept on growing, right through the day, till I was well past being Michael Owen and half-way to being King of the World. Teachers, caretakers and dinner ladies all seemed unbelievably tedious and tiny-minded. Nothing mattered but the match against St Peter's.

By the time the match actually began I was like a dragster on the start-line. I laced my shoes in silent concentration, completely unaware of my team-mates around me. Then, at the first sight of the St Peter's boys, I simply went mental. I marched straight up to the biggest lad and stuck my forehead to his.

"You up for it?" I said. "I'm mad for it, me!"

Mr Bollom looked up in amazement. But I wasn't finished yet. I flew round the gym, belting balls against the walls, yelling, "Mad for it! Mad for it!" Then I decided our team should do a war chant, like the All Blacks.

The others stood round open-mouthed as I stamped my feet and slapped my forearms, chanting, "Hama-tay! Hama-tay!" and all kinds of other gobbledegook which flowed freely from my mouth without the least advice from my brain.

"Joseph," said Mr Bollom, sternly. "Calm down, will you?"

"Got you, chief."

The truth was, I had no intention of calming down, and when the whistle went off, so did I. I ran and span like a whirling dervish. I could sense terror in the St Peter's boys any time I got near them. No one would tackle me. I ran clean through at least six times to hammer the ball into an empty net. The match seemed to last about five minutes, and we won by a hatful. The St Peter's lads trudged away, casting resentful glances in my direction.

Mr Bollom grabbed my arm the moment I left the gym and took me into the equipment room.

"Joseph," he said. "Enthusiasm is all very well. But you were completely over the top!"

"We won," I replied, "didn't we?"

"What matters," said Mr Bollom, "is the manner in which you play the game."

"Football," I replied, "is not a matter of life and death. It's much more important than that." That sounded good, I thought, even if I'd heard it somewhere before.

"I am the manager of this team," said Mr Bollom, "and unless you get a grip on yourself, you will not be playing for it again. Is that understood?"

"Yo, chief."

"Yes. Sir."

"Yo, sir."

"I mean it, Joseph. Next time you clog an opponent, you're out."

"I read you, Captain."

The truth was I had hardly heard a word old Bollom had said. I practically danced all the way home and as I waltzed through the front door I was still buzzing.

Mum was in the front room having one of her afternoon socials. Mum liked to invite the most boring people in town for tea and drag out her best Royal Doulton cups. Today it was a small blue woman with a bent back and a little twisted smile.

"Joseph!" said Mum, "come in and meet Mrs Betty, the chairwoman of the Townswomen's Guild."

I lurched into the room. "Yo, Miss Betty!" I said, "how's it hanging?"

Mum's face dropped.

"Would you like a fairy cake?" offered Mrs Betty.

"On me head then!"

"I beg your pardon?"

"On me head!"

Suddenly, I felt my arm in Mum's tiger-paw

grip. Next second we were in the kitchen.

"You cheeky…"

Mum searched for the worst swear word she could think of.

"…so-and-so!"

"Just being friendly," I replied.

Mum's eyes suddenly narrowed. "Your eyes look funny," she said.

I quickly looked away. "It's genetic," I said. "I get them from you."

Mum turned my head back towards her, frowning hard. I gave a laugh, slipped free, and made for the safety of my bedroom.

Now for the first time, I stopped and took a deep breath. A little cloud of anxiety had appeared in my perfect blue sky. I walked in front of the dressing-table mirror and studied my eyes closely.

Wow! I thought. No wonder Mum was worried. My eyes were shot with blood and I had the face of a wild animal.

A wave of panic came over me. I couldn't afford to make this mistake again. I had to flush that space rock down the toilet.

7
Out of the Team

I really did try. When it was obvious the space rock wouldn't flush away, I wrapped it in newspaper and put it at the bottom of a black bag, then covered it with rubbish. It sat out in the backyard for days, waiting for collection day, except there was a bank holiday which meant all the collections were late.

Meanwhile, my world was slowly going to pieces. I seemed to feel irritable all the time and couldn't do the simplest things right. Face it, Joe, I told myself. It's not just football you need help with. It's life in general.

I can't remember exactly when I decided to dig out the space rock. But I did it in the dead of night, in the pouring rain, the very night before the binmen were due. I should have felt defeated but I simply felt relieved. As I carried it back to my room all the cares seem to lift from my shoulders. Anyway, I told myself, what was wrong with feeling good? Wasn't that why Mum drank tea and Dad went into space?

No, I just had to make sure I didn't have too much next time. That way, the space rock wouldn't control me. I'd control the space rock.

* * *

I never meant to take it every day, but over the next week I soon found that I had to. Every morning I'd take out the space rock, then file off just enough to fill a medicine spoon. As soon as it had taken effect, I set off for school. The reason for this was that I soon found that without it I was getting steadily more useless. My body wouldn't seem to work right at all. I was cack-handed, ham-fisted and butterfingered. I couldn't catch a cold and I couldn't hit a cow with a banjo.

Anyway. Let's get on to what really mattered. What really mattered was that we were in the quarter-finals of the Schools' Cup and we were playing Bendal Green, last year's winners. People said that Bendal were unbeatable, and that all their players were twice as big as we were, and they did two hours basic skills every night. Not only that, but they had James Duff, the boy they called the Bendal Butcher. People said the Bendal Butcher had put three boys in casualty in this tournament alone.

I could sense the rest of the team was super-nervous at playing Bendal, and that included Cornel. As we sat in the changing rooms he'd already started making his excuses. "We're on a learning curve," he said. "Any defeat this year will make us stronger next year."

"But Cornel," I said, "we're not going to lose."

Cornel turned, anxiously. "I never said we

were going to lose," he said.

"Good," I replied.

We headed for the match, but I'd already won a little victory.

MATCH REPORT   *By Joseph Mellors*

MELLORS STARS AS STEGG END STEAL IT

Stegg End's remarkable Cup run goes on. This time their victims were none other than defending champions Bendal Green, humbled 14–10 on their own patch yesterday afternoon.

It was a see-saw match but one thing remained constant – Stegg End's Joseph Mellors. Mellors controlled the game with a series of pinpoint passes, intelligent use of space and some delightful one-twos, one of which set up Stegg End captain Cornel Smart for the first goal.

With five minutes to go, the teams were tied at ten-all. Then Mellors collected a ball from just outside his own goal area, set off on a mazy dribble (making excellent use of

---

the gym wall), pulled two defenders out of position, then back-heeled perfectly for Rachid Ahmed to crack the ball into the net.

It was the beginning of the end for Bendal Green, whose James Duff could only respond with a series of sickening challenges which resulted in a booking. The so-called "Bendal Butcher" was lucky to avoid being sent for an early shower. Surely no one can escape Stegg End in their quest for Cup glory?

Yes, it was a great victory. But I have missed one small detail from the report. The Bendal Butcher was not the only name in the referee's book. He'd hacked me that many times, I just had to pay him back. We were face-on. I clipped the ball to the right, rebounding it off the wall, then went to pass him on the left. I knew he was going to clog me. I saw his right leg come up, and with split-second timing I took his left one. He came down like a dump truck. The floor was still shaking after the final whistle.

Unfortunately, so was Mr Bollom.

"I warned you, Joseph!" he railed.

"You wouldn't drop me!" I laughed.

"Watch me," said Mr Bollom.

I looked into his eyes and saw he meant it.

* * *

Dad was waiting for me when I got home. Since I'd been in space with him he'd picked up this habit of winking at me every so often, and occasionally giving me a little friendly punch on the arm. But today there was no wink and no punch, just a serious expression.

"Your mum wants us to have a little chat," he said.

"Oh, yes?" I replied.

Silence. Dad got up and walked across the kitchen and into the garage. A few minutes passed, then his head appeared again.

"Come on then!" he said.

"You want me to follow?" I asked.

"What do you think?" said Dad.

As usual, we were communicating brilliantly. I went through to the garage and sat on the bench. Dad paced from side to side, looking at anything but me.

"Your mum's worried about you," he said, finally.

"Why?" I replied. "There's nothing wrong with me!"

"You were rude to Mrs Betty."

"I was friendly!"

"Your mother says you were rude."

"It was just a joke, Dad!"

"Anyway… there's other things."

"Such as?"

"Not eating properly."

"Honest, Dad! Mum thinks if you don't eat two cows a day you're anorexic!"

"Then there's these moods."

"What moods?"

"One day you're miserable, next day you're high as a kite."

"Pressure of modern life, Dad."

Dad put his hand in the vice and absentmindedly tightened it. "Is there anything... you need to tell me?" he blurted out.

I thought for a moment. "Yes, Dad," I murmured.

"Go on," said Dad.

"Mr Bollom's kicking me out of the team."

"Oh," said Dad.

Silence.

"Maybe that's why I'm acting strange!" I suggested.

Dad didn't seem to hear. His brain was in another place.

"You remember I told you about the first binmen they sent up?" he asked.

"Yes?"

"They were fired because… they became addicted to something."

At the word "addicted", my veins froze. What did Dad know? Did he think I was an

addict? OK, I liked space rock, but I wasn't an addict!

"Dad," I said, "I don't know what you're on about, but there's nothing wrong with me, and I've got a lot of homework to do, and I'd appreciate it if you'd get off my case!"

I jumped off the bench and marched out of the garage, leaving Dad struggling to get his hand out of the vice.

8

Panic

The school team for the semi-final was being announced the day before the game.

We were playing Alderman Bugthorpe, who'd put twenty-five past Our Blessed Lady in the quarter-finals. Not that I wanted to know who we were playing. Still, I couldn't stop myself going to the notice board to see who Bollom had put in my place.

> Cornel Smart (capt.)
> Rachid Ahmed
> Linton Fox
> Paul Hardaker
> Joseph Mellors

I rubbed my eyes and looked again. It really

was true. I was still in the team!

"You're lucky, Mellors," came a voice behind me.

I spun round. Cornel was standing there, with a half-smile on his face.

"He knew he couldn't drop me!" I said.

"Yeah," replied Cornel. "After I persuaded him."

"Honest?"

"I want to win this Cup," said Cornel.

* * *

When I got home I went straight up to my room. I wanted to get everything ready for the next day. I laid out my kit and packed my bag. Then I took my medicine spoon from my pencil case and the nail file from under the bed. Carefully and quietly, I eased open my desk drawer.

The space rock was not there.

I pulled all the paper out of the drawer. I checked all the corners. I checked the other drawers, just in case I'd put it there by mistake.

The space rock was nowhere.

Panic welled up in me. I felt like I was drowning, like all the breath had gone out of my lungs and all the blood from my heart. My head swam and my fingers grasped the front of my shirt.

"Mum!"

I rushed headlong downstairs, spilling Batcat out of the way. Mum was in the kitchen, emptying the dishwasher with that dreamy look she always seemed to wear.

"Have you been in my room?" I blared.

"Keep your voice down, Joseph," said Mum calmly. "What will the neighbours think?"

"Have you been in my room?"

Mum put down a small cream jug and folded her arms. "I go into your room every day," she said. "Someone has to tidy up the mess."

"Have you touched anything?"

"I have to touch things to tidy up, don't I?"

"Taken anything, I mean!"

"Such as?"

"Something personal."

Mum sighed. "I really can't help you unless you can be more specific," she said. "Is it a diary you're missing? A love letter?"

"I don't get love letters!"

"Well, I don't know that, do I? I haven't the faintest idea what you get up to."

Mum put on a little smile, but not a very happy one. It was an expression that really annoyed me. But I knew, and she knew, that I could do absolutely nothing about it.

* * *

That evening I turned my room upside-down. I knew for a fact that I'd left the space rock in the drawer, but I just had to make absolutely sure it wasn't in my wardrobe, or behind my printer, or at the bottom of the dirty washing basket.

Surprise, surprise. It wasn't.

The bins were next. I rummaged through the waste bin in the bathroom, the living room, the front room and the downstairs toilet. Then I rolled up my shirt sleeves and got stuck into the bin in the kitchen.

I felt my way through leftover spag bol, rancid milk cartons and the remains of a chicken carcass. My hand came out stinking of stale tea and dripping with pork fat. But no space rock.

The dustbins were next. I pulled out the black bags and emptied them on to a sheet of cardboard. Another waste of time.

By now my face was sticky with sweat and there was an aching feeling in my guts. But there was no way I was giving up. If it hadn't been thrown it away, it had to be in the house.

But where?

I pictured all the rooms in the house. There were plenty of places you could hide a small piece of rock, but only one drawer with a lock on it. That was Mum's drawer in the bathroom.

So, where would she hide the key? It would have to be somewhere I'd never go, nor Dad, nor my little brothers Jacob and Jonah, whom I haven't mentioned before because, frankly, they're not important to the story.

Of course! The one place we'd never look! In the kitchen cupboard with the ironing board!

Two minutes later, the magic key was in my hand.

* * *

I checked the living room. Dad was asleep in front of the telly with a half-empty bottle of whisky by his side. Mum was making notes for her evening class in dog obedience. Mum had been taking these classes for six months, despite the fact we had no dog or anything like one. She had heard that a lot of the Best People went there and it was a good place to Make Connections.

Good, I thought to myself. Keep working, Mum. I've got a little detective work to do.

I crept upstairs, pushed open the door of the bathroom and slipped inside. There was a heavy smell of air freshener. Everything was so perfectly tidy it could have been a museum.

Heart thumping, I homed in on the secret drawer. How many times had I wondered what treasures lay inside there! Exotic chocolates, or diamond jewellery, or a little ancient sea chest full of gold doubloons!

I put in the key, turned, and eased the drawer open.

There were no chocolates, jewels, gold doubloons, or space rock. Just a wonderland of pills, fifteen bottles at least.

I studied the labels: Torzac, Parapaxol, Fruzepan. They sounded sinister, like *Star Trek* villains. Some were small, white and shiny, some were like big pink Smarties, and others were pretty two-coloured capsules.

Ha, I thought to myself. How can Mum tell me what not to take? She had enough chemicals there to open a chemist's shop!

9
The Semi-final

Next morning, the world came to an end. There is no word that describes how bad I felt.

I put a sheet of paper on the desk, took out the drawer, then swept all the dust out of it with a pastry brush. There was about half a thimble full. In amongst the fluff, the pencil lead and the dead skin cells there were surely a few specks of space dust.

I took a deep breath and licked the lot up. Then I collected my kit and set off for school.

* * *

There was no change in my condition by the end of assembly, which was when Mr Bollom collared me. "You've been very lucky, Joseph," he said sternly. "I hope you will repay my faith in you."

There was no change by last lesson. My legs were like lead and my head was filled with cotton wool. I gazed blankly through the classroom window as Alderman Bugthorpe's minibus arrived and six keen-looking kids with kitbags climbed out. They were all better than me, I knew it. And as I thought it, a sharp pain spread all the way up my body and settled in my left eye.

The bell. I picked up my bag and walked like a zombie to the changing rooms. Cornel greeted me. "All right, Joey?"

No one had ever called me "Joey" before, and I couldn't remember suggesting it to Cornel. But I wasn't up to arguing.

"Bit sick," I replied.

"We'll kill 'em," said Cornel. "No worries."

The others arrived. When we were all ready, Cornel got everyone's attention. "I just want to say something," he said.

Cornel glanced at me. Oh no, I thought.

"Mr Bollom says we've all got to play for each other," continued Cornel. "And that includes me and Joey. I know I've slagged him off, but the fact is, we wouldn't be here without Joey. So I don't mind admitting I was wrong, and that Joey's a wicked player. In fact… almost as good as me!"

Cornel punched my arm, everyone laughed, and I forced a very strained smile on to my face.

* * *

I'm not sure when the team first realized there was something wrong with me. I think it was probably the first time I touched the ball. I was standing just outside their goal area with no defender in sight. Cornel rolled the ball across to me, I took aim, missed completely, and fell on my butt.

It was probably the highlight of my game. At least I was somewhere near the ball. Other than that, it really was like one of those nightmares when someone's after you and you can't force your legs to move. The game went on all around me but I wasn't part of it.

Everyone seemed so fast, so sharp, so determined. Soon my own team started getting down on me, moaning, "Oh Mellors!" like the bad old days.

Eventually they cut me out altogether. I was like a sick old man groping around in a world of confusion. The bright lights and the loud shouts became more and more unreal, until I began to lose it altogether.

I lost all sense of where I was and what I was doing there. I vaguely remember Mr Bollom taking my arm and asking if I was all right. Leaving the gym. Getting dressed. Sitting alone on the playground wall in the dark, with fifty screaming devils scrambling to get out of my head. Trudging home in a cloud of shame with nothing to look forward to but sleep.

10
Into Space

When I heard Stegg End had won the semi-final, I laughed. This was the cruellest trick of all. The greatest prize was right before me and I was terrified.

I had to play, I knew that. The thought of Adrian Keele or Billy Todd taking my place was too much to bear. I made up some story about this illness I'd got, called soccer flu, a mystery virus which only affected attacking midfielders. Mr Bollom didn't swallow that one so I told him I'd been over-training and it had weakened my immune system.

"Hmm," he said, "and what if this mystery illness is still affecting you by the time of the final?"

"Mr Bollom," I said, "I swear on my life, cross my heart and hope to die, I will play good in the final."

Mr Bollom thought long and hard before telling me I would have to prove my fitness, just like the England crocks do.

*　*　*

For a while, I fooled myself that I could make the grade without any help from space rock. I decided to practise, like the old days, when I'd take shots at the back wall for hours on end. But no sooner had I started than a terrible feeling of hopelessness came over me. The little energy I'd got drained out of my legs, and the ball rolled weakly into a ditch. I went back inside and sat on my bed. An hour passed, maybe two, and still I hadn't moved. I was like one of those sad husks you see in old people's homes.

There was only one thing for it. I had to get

some more of that stuff. I didn't care if I had to beg, borrow or steal. It didn't even matter if I had to creep to Dad.

"Dad," I said, trying to sound bright and breezy, "I've made a decision."

"Yes?" said Dad, suspiciously.

"I'm going to follow in your footsteps, Dad. I'm going to be a binman."

Dad reached forward and patted me awkwardly on the elbow. "You're a good lad," he said.

Pause.

"So," I said. "When are we going up again?"

Dad shook his head. "That was a once-off," he said.

"You've got to let me come up again!" I pleaded.

"Impossible," said Dad. "They've tightened security."

"We'll get past them!"

"Too risky."

"Just one more time!"

"Joseph. I said NO."

I stormed from the room, slamming the door, and then slammed my bedroom door for good measure. As I slumped on to the bed, Batcat appeared from nowhere and jumped on to my lap, purring. I pushed her off. She jumped up again. I pushed her off again. She jumped up again.

"For Pete's sake!"

I thwacked Batcat with a full-force backhand. She mewled in pain, leaped away and scurried off to hide. I watched blankly, too obsessed with my own problems to feel guilt.

All right, I thought to myself. If Dad won't take me into space, there's only one solution. I'll get there on my own.

* * *

I planned everything for Saturday morning. I knew the binmen never worked Saturdays, unless it was after a bank holiday, so the Star Cart would be on its launch pad and there would be no one around. To make absolutely sure of this, I set my alarm for half-past four.

I had everything packed and ready, even some pies and a can of Alien Cola.

As usual I felt dreadful when I woke up. My back ached and my head was full of a strange sense of doom. I dragged myself into my clothes and picked up my bag, which felt unusually heavy. Then again, maybe my arms were unusually weak.

I set out into the dark morning, with only the owls and foxes for company. It was a long, long walk to the council depot and my bag seemed to grow heavier with every step. It was cold as well. I had a vague idea that you shouldn't launch rockets below a certain temperature. They tended to explode and atomise everyone on board.

At last, the gates. Locked, of course. I slung my bag across my shoulder and climbed over. Immediately, a security light came on. I ran like an animal past the dark shadows of the refuse vans towards the faceless corrugated wall of Shed Number Seven.

One… nine… six… six…

Open Sesame!

Everything was as I remembered it. The Star Cart, monstrous in the half-light. The space overalls. The goldfish-bowl helmets. I dressed myself hurriedly and searched through the pockets of Charlie's overalls for the keys. Where were they?

I shook the overalls hard. Out dropped fifty pence, and an organ donor card. *In the event of my death...*, I didn't read any further. Just shook the overalls harder. This time, a set of keys clinked to the floor. I seized them as if they were pure gold. I was in business.

Five minutes later, the ignition key was in place and I was building up the courage to turn it. But it was not bravery which forced me to do it, just sheer desperation. The engine fired, the roof opened, and that invisible elephant sat back on my face. No going back now.

I concentrated on the windscreen, trying to stop myself from thinking too much. I reminded myself I was on a mission, and at the end of it, everything would be all right again. I would clutch a whole pile of space rocks to my heart and I would feel safe and secure and able to face the world. The Cup Final would be the greatest day of my life and I would be carried around the playground with the whole school chanting my name and Mr Bollom asking for my autograph.

Yes, it would be a wonderful, fearless world where the sun shone every day, and everybody lived forever. School books would be made of chocolate and instead of writing in them you ate them, and teachers would give a merit mark to the biggest pig.

Time passed. Space passed. I tried playing solo hangman and making up my all-time World Soccer XI. Then I started working on my all-time *Star Trek* crew, but it only reminded me of how alone I was.

Suddenly in the far distance, a little cloud appeared. My heart leapt. Space rock! It had to be space rock! Full steam ahead! Warp Factor Five!

Star Cart Enterprise and the shower of meteorites rushed to embrace each other. Time was short. I took off my seatbelt, floated to the back of the cab and pulled out a lifeline. So far so good. It was just a matter of attaching the line to the suit…

How did the line attach to the suit?

My fingers fumbled desperately. For the life of me, I could not work out how the connection was made.

"Dad!" I wailed. "Where are you?"

I tried pushing, twisting, popping, screwing and zipping. I tried smacking the lifeline against the wall and screaming swear words at it. Inside the spacesuit my body was getting hotter and hotter and the sweat was dripping into my eyes.

The space rocks were almost upon us.

Close enough to see that magical pink glimmer. Almost close enough to taste.

"Come on!"

I made one last frenzied attempt on the lifeline, but my arms were so tired they would hardly work any more. And then, at last, something clicked.

"Yes!" I cried.

I glanced up at the windscreen. Nothing but stars.

I hurried to the exit bay. Inner door… outer door… out!

But my efforts were all in vain. I had taken too long. The cloud of space rocks was vanishing into infinity.

Devastated, I stumbled back into the cab and collapsed. Tears of frustration bubbled up. For a millisecond I thought about chasing the rocks, but when I looked at the fuel gauge, I knew it would mean almost certain death. The needle was pointing just above nil, and getting home was an urgent priority.

It was now that the real nightmare began. All the thoughts I'd been holding back suddenly burst through, and I was swept away in a tide of doubts and fears. There was no way I could call Mum, pick up the phone, or turn on the radio. I was completely responsible for myself, except I wasn't responsible at all. I was an addict, just like Dad said. There was no point in pretending any more.

My fingers clutched at the console. All around me were rattles, beeps and buzzes. It was as if the Star Cart was a living organism and I was its victim.

And now the most terrible thought of all came to me: I was hurtling at five thousand miles an hour towards the Earth's atmosphere, and I had no idea how to enter it.

I stared blankly at the computer, remembering Charlie's words: "Get the angle too steep, you'll burn to a cinder... Get it too flat, you'll bounce off into space forever". If only I could think clearly!

I stabbed at a few keys. I managed to bring up Word for Windows and half my breakfast.

"Help!" I cried.

There was no one to listen.

"Please!" I pleaded. "I just want to go back to normal! I don't care if I play for the reserves! It's only a game, after all!"

My head hit the console and my eyes fell on my bag. It was then I noticed the most sinister thing of all.

My bag was moving!

First it lurched to the left side. Then a lurch to the right. Then it fell over.

Suddenly I remembered how heavy it had felt.

With trembling fingers I reached for the zip. Slowly I eased it back… and out climbed Batcat.

* * *

"It's you!" I cried.

Batcat stretched, yawned, arched her back and offered her chin. Without thinking, I tickled it. Something in this comforting, everyday ritual brought me back to my senses. Even in space, her movements were sure and her concentration was total. *That is how I must be*, I told myself.

I smoothed Batcat's head, studied her face, then turned to the computer console. Somewhere, from the back of my mind, I dredged up a memory of Charlie. I tapped a few keys, and, like a miracle, the magic words appeared before me: RE-ENTRY PROGRAMME.

I had to work fast. I typed in our co-ordinates, speed, and fuel status. Then I activated the atmospheric probes and placed the Star Cart on what I prayed was the perfect trajectory.

Now we waited, for a happy return, or oblivion.

Suddenly, wonderfully, the beautiful blue Earth appeared in a graceful curve before us. Then we were sailing safely down between the clouds, and I was breathing a long, luxurious sigh of relief.

Mission accomplished. I turned back to

Batcat, who was casually licking her tail.

"We did it, puss," I said, smoothing her coat and gazing into those powerful eyes, untouched by pills, alcopops or space rock, high on the pure joy of life.

11

Freedom

It was the proudest moment of my life when Cornel lifted the five-a-side Cup. We all kissed it like it was the World Cup itself, then squatted for the cameras, jigging and singing like they do at Wembley.

That night, safe in bed, I replayed my winning goal over and over in my mind. Storming out of defence in a two-man commando raid. Ball bouncing back and forth like a pinball between me and Cornel, defenders like dazed flies. Hammering it towards the far corner, seeing it ricochet off the goalie, pouncing like a wildcat, shaping to smash it, then caressing it the other way.

Then, finally, watching it nestle softly into the back of the net like a dream, like all my hopes coming to fruit.

So, you ask, how did I do it? How did I

play so brilliantly without a whiff of space rock?

I can only find one answer. I felt strong. After all, I had just cheated death. But there was something even more important. I had conquered my weakness. I did not need space rock. I was free again, apart from the fact that Mum, school and the government were still telling me what to do.

As for my addiction to football... now that really was a problem.

About the author

I was brought up in Southampton and decided to be a writer when I was about five. My newspaper, *World Times*, was featured on Southern Television when I was nine, and I was very embarrassed about it.

My first novel was published in 1986 and since then I've written about thirty books. I have also had proper jobs, like selling shoes and teaching at university. I now live in Cardiff and I do have a cat, who is rather similar to Batcat.

The ideas for *Space Rock and Five-a-Side* came from all over the place – I started with the idea of a space dustman, then thought I'd write about football, which I used to love playing. Like most of my stories, it is meant to be funny and serious at the same time.